New CLAIT 2006

Unit 5
Creating an e-Presentation

Using
Microsoft® PowerPoint 2007

Release NC639v1

Published by:

CiA Training Ltd
Business & Innovation Centre
Sunderland Enterprise Park
Sunderland SR5 2TH
United Kingdom

Tel: +44 (0)191 549 5002
Fax: +44 (0)191 549 9005

E-mail: info@ciatraining.co.uk
Web: www.ciatraining.co.uk

ISBN 13: 978-1-86005-484-6

Important Note

This guide was written using *Windows Vista*. If using *Windows XP* some dialog boxes will look different, although the content is the same.

A screen resolution of 1024 x 768 was used. Working in a different screen resolution, or with an application window which is not maximised, will change the look of the *Office 2007* Ribbon.

The ribbon appearance is dynamic, it changes to fit the space available. The full ribbon may show a group containing several options, but if space is restricted it may show a single button that you need to click to see the same options, e.g. the

Editing group may be replaced by the **Editing** button.

First published 2007

Copyright © 2007 CiA Training Ltd

CIA Training's guides for **New CLAIT 2006** are a collection of structured exercises to provide support for each unit in the new qualification. The exercises build into a complete open learning package covering the entire syllabus, to teach how to use a particular software application. They are designed to take the user through the features to enhance, fulfil and instil confidence in the product. The accompanying data enables the user to practise new techniques without the need for data entry.

UNIT 5: CREATING AN e-PRESENTATION - The guide supporting this unit contains exercises covering the following topics:

- Creating Presentations
- Views
- Adding Slides
- Running Presentations
- Text Effects
- Slide Master
- Applying Backgrounds

- Demote and Promote Text
- Saving Presentations
- Inserting Pictures
- Text Formatting
- Printing
- Clip Art
- Bullets

*Visit **www.ciasupport.co.uk** for hints, tips and supplementary information on published CiA products.*

This guide is suitable for:

- Any individual wishing to sit the OCR examination for this unit. The user works through the guide from start to finish.

- Tutor led groups as reinforcement material. It can be used as and when necessary.

Aims and Objectives

To provide the knowledge and techniques necessary for the attainment of a certificate in this unit. After completing the guide the user will be able to:

- identify and use presentation graphics software correctly
- set up a slide layout
- select fonts and enter text
- format slides
- manage and print presentation files

Downloading the Data Files

The data associated with these exercises must be downloaded from our website. Go to: **www.ciatraining.co.uk/data**. Follow the on screen instructions to download the appropriate data files.

By default, the data files will be downloaded to **Documents\CIA DATA FILES\New CLAIT 2006\Unit 5 PowerPoint 2007 Data** (Note: *Windows XP* downloads to a **My Documents** folder).

If you prefer, the data can be supplied on CD at an additional cost. Contact the Sales team at **info@ciatraining.co.uk**.

Introduction

This guide was created using version *2007* of *PowerPoint*. It assumes that the programs have been correctly and **fully** installed on your personal computer. Some features described in this guide may not work if the program was not **fully** installed.

Notation Used Throughout This Guide

- Key presses are included within < > e.g. **<Enter>** means press the Enter key.

- The guide is split into individual exercises. Each exercise consists of a written explanation of the feature, followed by a stepped exercise. Read the **Guidelines** and then follow the **Actions**, with reference to the **Guidelines** if necessary.

Recommendations

- Work through the exercises in sequence so that one feature is understood before moving on to the next.

- Read the whole of each exercise before starting to work through it. This ensures the understanding of the topic and prevents unnecessary mistakes.

PowerPoint 2007

New CLAIT

Section 1

Fundamentals

By the end of this Section you should be able to:

Understand *PowerPoint* Principles

Start *PowerPoint*

Recognise the Screen Layout

Open a Presentation

Run a Presentation

Close a Presentation

Exit *PowerPoint*

Exercise 1 - Starting PowerPoint

Guidelines:

PowerPoint is a powerful presentation graphics application, which allows impressive presentations to be produced with ease. Presentations can be viewed on screen, on an overhead projector, on 35mm slides, or as web pages.

A presentation can include text in any format, pictures, graphs, tables, organisation charts, sound and video. A finished slide show can incorporate animation and special effects.

Presentation notes, handouts, slide printouts and text outlines can also be produced.

Although there are numerous ways to start the program, the following method is recommended for beginners.

Actions:

1. When the computer is started, the *Windows* **Desktop** is automatically shown. Click once on the **Start** button, , in the bottom left corner of the screen, to show the list of options available.

2. Move to **All Programs** and then click **Microsoft Office**.

> Games
> Maintenance
> Microsoft Office
>   Microsoft Office Access 2007
>   Microsoft Office Excel 2007
>   Microsoft Office InfoPath 2007
>   Microsoft Office Outlook 2007
>   Microsoft Office PowerPoint 2007
>   Microsoft Office Publisher 2007
>   Microsoft Office Word 2007
>   Microsoft Office Tools

3. Click Microsoft Office PowerPoint 2007. The application will open and the screen will appear similar to the diagram on the next page.

Exercise 2 - The PowerPoint Screen and Ribbon

Guidelines:

In previous versions of *Microsoft Office* applications, commands were controlled by a series of menus and toolbars. *PowerPoint 2007* has replaced these with a **Ribbon** which is displayed at the top of the application window. The **Ribbon** contains buttons and drop down lists to control the operation of *PowerPoint*. The Ribbon is divided into a series of **Tabs**, each one of which has a set of controls specific to a certain function or process. On each tab, the controls are further divided into separate **Groups** of connected functions.

Some tabs can be selected manually, some only appear when certain operations are active, for example only when a **Chart** is active, will **Chart Tools** tabs be displayed on the Ribbon.

Above the Ribbon is the **Quick Access Toolbar** which contains a few popular command buttons. By default this toolbar has three buttons, **Save**, **Undo** and **Repeat**. This toolbar can be customised by adding further buttons. The screen should be similar to the diagram below. Work through the following steps to locate the features.

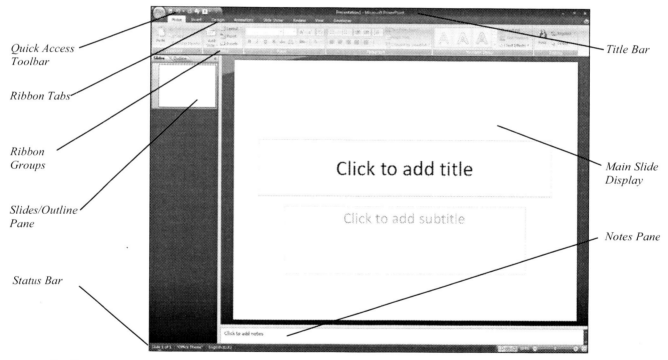

Actions:

1. Look at the top line, the **Title Bar**, displays **Microsoft PowerPoint**. It also shows the title of the current presentation, **Presentation1**

2. On the left of the **Title Bar** is the **Quick Access Toolbar**. By default this toolbar has three buttons. Place the cursor on each button in turn and read the **ToolTip** for each.

continued over

Exercise 2 - Continued

3. The third button can have a dual function. This button changes to a **Redo** button after the **Undo** button has been used, but at other times it can be the **Repeat** button.

*Note: The text in the **ToolTip** after the **Undo** and **Repeat** button names will vary according to the actions you perform.*

4. To the right of the **Repeat** button is the **Customize Quick Access Toolbar** button, ⬚. This is used to add new commands to the toolbar. This will not be used in this unit.

5. Below the **Title Bar** is the **Ribbon**, where commands are chosen using the mouse. It is made up of **Tabs** (the words at the top of the ribbon, which illuminate when the mouse is rolled over them), **Groups** (the boxes which spread horizontally across the ribbon, distinguishable by their names at the bottom of each) and **Commands** (the icons within groups which perform different actions).

6. Find the bar at the bottom of the screen. This is called the **Status Bar**, where the slide number and template design will be displayed.

7. The main part of the screen shows various views of the current presentation. The default view, shown here is **Normal View**.

8. On the **Ribbon**, the **Home** tab should be selected. Other tabs are available.

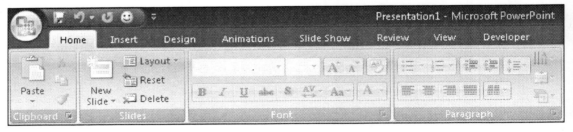

Part of the Ribbon displaying the Home tab

Note: Any buttons displayed in pale grey are called ghosted and are not available to be selected at present.

9. Notice how the buttons on the **Ribbon** are divided into **Groups** (**Clipboard**, **Slides**, **Font**, etc.).

*Note: The display of buttons on the **Ribbon** is dynamic. That is it will change according to how much space there is available. If the window is not maximised or the screen resolution is anything other than 1024 by 768, the Ribbon will not always appear as shown in this guide.*

10. Leave the cursor over any the buttons. A **ToolTip** appears which give more information and an alternative key press for the function if available.

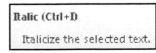

continued over

Exercise 2 - Continued

11.   Some buttons produce immediate effects, like the **Bold**, **Italic** and **Underline** buttons in the **Font** group.

12.   Buttons with a drop down arrow lead to further options. In the **Editing** group, click the **Replace** button drop down arrow, 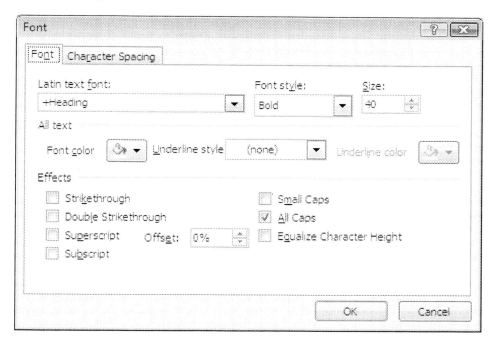. A list of further options is displayed.

13.   Some options will display a dialog box which needs data to be entered. Click the first option **Replace**, the **Replace** dialog box is displayed. Click the **Close** button in the dialog box to remove it.

14.   On the slide click in the **Click to add title** box and type **Introduction**.

15.   Some groups have a dialog box launcher to the right of the group name, e.g. the **Font** group,

16.   With your cursor on the word **Introduction** in the slide, click the **Font** dialog box launcher, , to the right of the **Font** group name, to display the **Font** dialog box.

17.   This is a tabbed dialog box, similar to those used in previous versions. Click **Cancel** to close the **Font** dialog box.

18.   Display the other **Ribbon** tabs, one at a time, **Insert**, **Design**, **Animations**, **Slide Show**, etc., to see which other commands are available.

19.   Click the **Home** tab again.

Exercise 3 - Opening a Presentation

Guidelines:

A presentation is made up of a series of **slides** that can be shown on screen or printed out. Once created and saved, a presentation can be opened at any time.

Actions:

1. Click the **Office Button**, and then click .

2. The **Open** dialog box appears. Make sure that the **Files of type** box at the bottom shows **All PowerPoint Presentations**.

3. The **Documents** folder is automatically shown. Double click on **CIA DATA FILES**, then on **New CLAIT 2006**, then on **Unit 5 PowerPoint Data** to display the contents of the supplied data folder (*see Note on Page 4*).

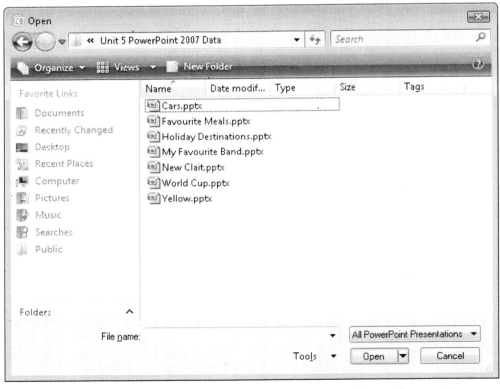

Note: *The files may be displayed differently to the picture above, depending on the* ***Views*** *setting. The picture above is shown in* ***Small Icons*** *view.*

4. Select **New Clait** from the list of files and click .

5. Leave the presentation open for the next exercise.

Exercise 4 - Slide Show Basics

Guidelines:

The best way to see what *PowerPoint* is capable of is to view a completed presentation.

The **Slide Show** is used to preview the presentation. The show will start from the slide currently being viewed.

Strictly speaking, running the presentation is not part of the New CLAIT syllabus, however, it will help you understand how a presentation looks and how it can be used.

Presentations should follow certain guidelines, or **conventions**. As the show runs, notice how each slide has an identical background. The bullet points are in the same style and there are a similar number on each page. It is important to have consistency like this in a presentation; it gives the information more impact when the viewer is not bombarded with a different style and colour on each slide.

Actions:

Note: *Before starting this exercise, you need to make sure the default settings have not been changed on your computer. Click the* **Office Button** *and then click* **PowerPoint Options**. *Select* **Advanced** *from the left of the window. From the* **Slide Show** *area at the right, make sure* ☑ End with black slide *is checked and click* **OK**.

1. Using the presentation opened in the previous exercise, click the **Slide Show** tab on the **Ribbon**.

2. Click the **From Beginning** button in the **Start Slide Show** group. The slide show starts, with the first slide filling the screen.

Note: *The* **Slide Show** *button,* 🖵*, at the right of* **Taskbar** *can be used to start a slide show.*

3. The slide show has been saved in such a way that you need to do nothing else until it ends. When the end of the show is reached, a black screen appears, with the words **End of slide show, click to exit**.

4. Click once with the left mouse button and the screen returns to showing all the slides in miniature.

5. Leave the presentation on screen for the next exercise.

Exercise 5 - Closing a Presentation

Guidelines:

To clear the screen and begin working on a new presentation, the current one can be closed. If the presentation has not been previously saved, or if it has been modified in any way, a prompt to save it will appear.

Actions:

1. The **New Clait** presentation should still be on the screen.

2. Click the **Office Button** and click **Close**. No changes have been made to the presentation, so no saving is required.

3. The **New Clait** presentation closes <u>without</u> any prompt.

4. The previous presentation with the text **Introduction** that was added is still open. Close **Presentation1**. Because this presentation has not yet been saved there will be a prompt.

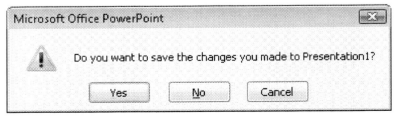

5. At the message prompt, click **No** to close without saving.

Exercise 6 - Exiting PowerPoint

Guidelines:

When *PowerPoint* is closed, if any presentations are still open and have not been saved, a warning will be displayed with an option to save the changes.

Actions:

1. There should be no presentations open. The centre of the screen should be blank. If there are any presentations open close them.

2. Click the **Office Button** to reveal the options.

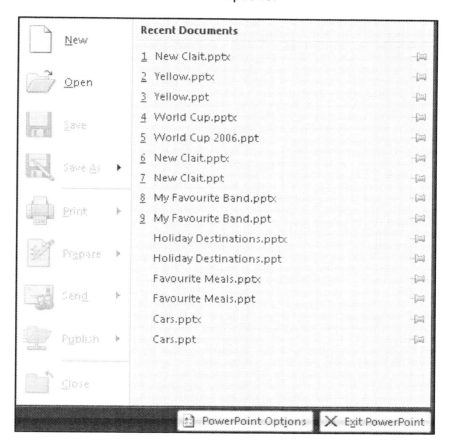

3. Place the mouse pointer over the **Exit PowerPoint** button and click once.

Note: *PowerPoint can also be closed by clicking the* **Close** *button,* ☒ *, in the top right corner of the screen.*

Exercise 7 - Revision

1. Open *PowerPoint 2007*.

2. Select **Open** from the **Office Button** options.

3. Locate the data files for this unit.

4. Select **My Favourite Band** and open it.

5. Run the slide show. Once again this show has been saved so that nothing needs to be done during the show.

6. Close the presentation.

Section 2

Slide Views

By the end of this Section you should be able to:

Understand and Use Different Views

Save and Close Presentations

Exercise 8 - Views

Guidelines:

There are different ways to view a presentation on screen in *PowerPoint*. Each view shows a different aspect of the presentation. The views are:

Normal View   Combines the **Main Slide Display** with optionally a **Slides/Outline Pane** on the left and a **Notes Pane** at the bottom. Each area of the screen can be resized individually.

Slide Sorter View   The whole presentation is displayed as a series of slide miniatures. Useful for previewing a presentation and to change the order, effects and timings of the slide show.

Slide Show   Used to view presentations in their final form, with animations and audio if appropriate.

Notes Page View   Each page has a slide image on the top with space to create and view speaker's notes below. These notes can also be seen in a pane at the bottom of **Normal View**.

Slides/Outline Pane   This pane on the left of **Normal** View has two tabs. The **Slides** tab shows a vertical list of slide miniatures, useful for navigating and previewing. The **Outline** tab shows a list of the text content of the slides. Used to manipulate text in a presentation, including the option to promote/demote text.

Actions:

1.   Click the **Office Button** and select **Open** to display the **Open** dialog box.

2.   Select the presentation **My Favourite Band** and click **Open**. This presentation opens in **Slide Sorter View**.

3.   Display the **View** tab. The view options are listed in the **Presentation Views** group.

4.   Click the **Normal** button. The first slide is displayed with the **Slides/Outline** pane on the left. The **Slides** tab is displayed by default.

5.   Click the **Outline** tab. The slides are shown as text. This view is used to add or edit the presentation page titles and text. Click the **Slides** tab to display **Slides** miniatures again.

6.   Click the **Notes Page** button on the **Ribbon**. This view is used to create speaker's notes for the slides, in the bottom half of the screen.

Note: *There are two view buttons, **Normal** and **Slide Sorter** to the left of the **Slide Show** button on the right side of the **Status Bar**.*

Normal   Slide Sorter   Slide Show

7.   Leave the presentation on screen for the next exercise.

Exercise 9 - Using Normal View

Guidelines:

The main slide display within **Normal View** shows the presentation slides, one at a time, in almost full screen size, with all text properly formatted and with a background or theme. The scroll bar at the right of the screen can be used to move from one slide to another.

Actions:

1. With the presentation still on screen, click the **Normal** button.

2. Click the **Next Slide** button, ![Next Slide], at the bottom of the vertical scroll bar, to move to the next slide.

3. Click the **Previous Slide** button, ![Previous Slide], to move back one slide.

4. Click and hold the scroll button down to view a grey caption, indicating the current slide.

5. Click and drag the scroll button and release the mouse when the marker for the third slide, **UK Tour**, appears.

6. Press <**Ctrl Home**> to move to the first slide in the presentation. Press <**Ctrl End**> to move to the last slide in the presentation.

7. Practise moving through the slides in **Slides** view, then return to slide **1**.

8. The pane at the left of the screen provides another option for moving between slides. Click on slide **3** in the **Slides Pane**. Slide **3** is immediately displayed in the main slide display.

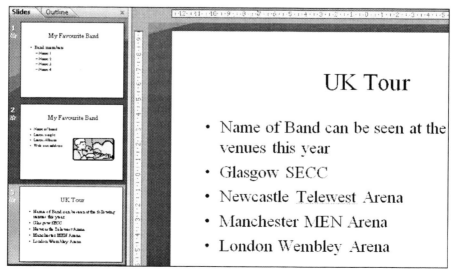

9. Leave the presentation on screen for the next exercise.

Exercise 10 - Using Slide Sorter View

Guidelines:

> **Slide Sorter View** shows all slides in a presentation on screen at the same time. This makes it easy to move, add or delete slides.

Actions:

1. With the presentation still on screen, click the **Slide Sorter** button. The screen will appear as below. Click and drag the slider on the **Zoom** control to change the size of the slides displayed.

2. When a presentation contains lots of slides, changing the zoom will display more or fewer slides. Change the **Zoom** back to **66%**.

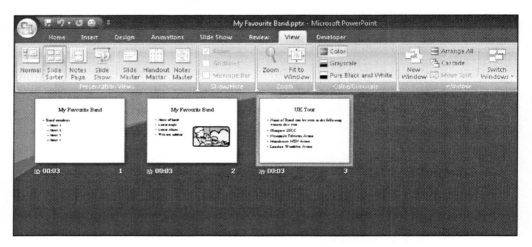

3. The numbers of the slides are shown beneath them and to the right. The selected slide has a coloured border around it. Click on each slide to display its border.

4. Click on the middle of slide number **3** and drag it left by holding down the left mouse button and moving the mouse in that direction. Notice that as the mouse pointer moves, an orange line appears, moving between slides.

5. Release the mouse button when the line is between slides **1** and **2**. When the mouse button is released, the line is replaced by the slide. The **UK Tour** slide now becomes slide **2**.

6. Leave the presentation on screen for the next exercise.

Exercise 11 - Saving an Edited Presentation

Guidelines:

Once a presentation has had changes made, then you need to decide if these changes are to be saved or not. Saving a presentation with the same filename will overwrite the original presentation; saving a presentation with a new filename will produce a new version, leaving the original presentation unaffected.

You should be aware of where the data associated with this guide is located. The file you are about to save should be saved to the same place (saving is explained in more detail in Exercise 19).

Actions:

1.   The **My Favourite Band** presentation should still be on the screen.

2.   Click the **Office Button** and then select **Save As**.

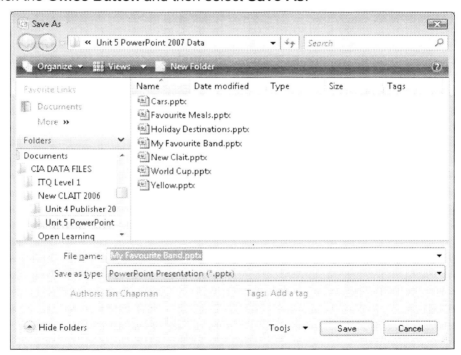

3.   At the dialog box, substitute the current **File name** with **My Band**.

Note: *This means that you will retain the original file (**My Favourite Band**) and produce a new copy with the changes you have just made (**My Band**).*

4.   The file will be saved in the folder shown at the top of the dialog box. Use the **Folders** list on the left to change this if it is not correct.

5.   Click the **Save** button, [Save].

6.   Click the **Office Button** and select **Close** to close the presentation.

Exercise 12 - Closing an Unsaved Presentation

Guidelines:

PowerPoint will display a warning if you attempt to close a presentation that contains any unsaved changes.

Actions:

1. Click the **Office Button** and then click **Open**.

2. Click on **My Favourite Band**.

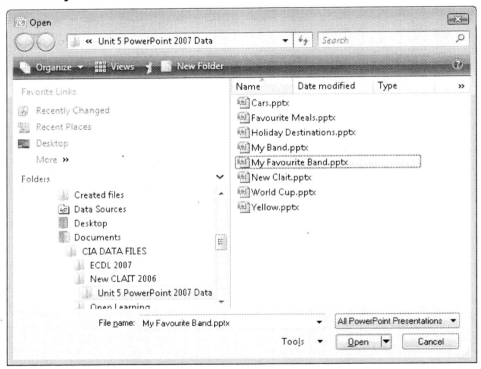

3. Click the **Open** button, 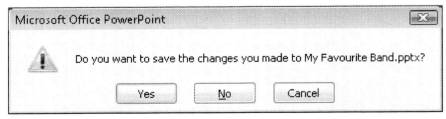.

4. In **Slide Sorter** view move the first slide to the end. The presentation has now been changed.

5. Click the **Office Button** and select **Close**. Because changes have been made, a prompt to save will appear.

continued over

Exercise 12 - Continued

6. Select **No**. This closes the presentation, <u>without</u> saving the changes that have been made.

Note: *If you had selected* **Yes** *at the prompt, the file would have been saved using the same file name.* **Cancel** *would return to the presentation.*

Exercise 13 - Revision

1. Open the presentation **New Clait**. Make sure you are in **Slide Sorter** view.

2. Use the **Zoom Slider** to change the magnification to **100%**. Some of the slides may now not be displayed on the screen.

3. Reduce the zoom so that all slides can be seen on the screen at once.

4. Move slide **10**, **Unit 8 - Online Communication**, so that it is displayed between slides **7** and **8**. It may take a moment for the slides to change. The slide numbers will be updated.

5. Click on the new slide number **10**. This should now be the slide referring to New CLAiT **Unit 7 - Web Pages**.

6. Save the changed presentation as **Unit 7**.

7. Close the presentation.

Exercise 14 - Revision

1. Open the presentation **My Band** saved in Exercise 11.

2. Move the **UK Tour** slide, so that it becomes slide number **3**.

3. Change to **Normal** view.

4. Use the scroll bar to move back to slide **1**.

5. Select **Slide 2** on the **Slides** pane to display it.

6. Close the presentation <u>without</u> saving.

Section 3

Presentations

By the end of this Section you should be able to:

Create a Blank Presentation

Use the Slide Master

Use Bullet Levels on Slides

Apply a Background

Save a Presentation

Add New Slides

Exercise 15 - Creating a Blank Presentation

Guidelines:

When creating a new blank presentation, a single blank slide will be shown, without colours, background, graphics, etc. All that has to be specified is the type of slide to be used, i.e. title slide, bulleted text, etc. The syllabus for **New CLAIT** only requires the use of slides with **Title and Content Layout**, which by default contains a title and a bulleted list of text.

Actions:

1. Click the **Office Button** and select **New** to display the **New Presentation** dialog box. Under **Blank and recent**, **Blank Presentation** will be selected. Click the **Create** button to start a new blank presentation.

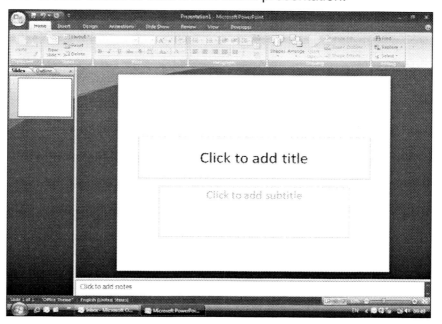

2. A **Title Slide** should be displayed by default. Display the **Home** tab and click the **Layout** button, from the **Slides** group.

3. The various available layouts are displayed. Select different layouts to see how the view in the main slide display changes. Finally select the **Title and Content** layout.

4. A completely blank presentation slide has been created with the layout of **Title and Content**. Text can be added to the boxes as indicated.

5. From the **Normal** view, any aspect of the presentation, such as background, text style, etc. can be defined.

6. Leave the blank presentation on screen for the next exercise.

Note: More usually, presentations start with a **Title Slide** to introduce the presentation.

Exercise 16 - Using Slide Master

Guidelines:

There are three types of master slides: **Slide**, **Handout** and **Notes**. The **Slide Master** allows the same text or graphics to be added to every slide in a presentation using **Master Slides**.

Each type of layout can have its own **Master Slide**, but the only one that is required for this qualification is the main **Master Slide** which defines the appearance of every slide in the presentation. The **Handout** and **Notes Masters** allow the same text or graphics to be added to all the notes and handouts accompanying the presentation.

Some establishments may use the same **Slide Master** for all of their presentations. You should find out if this happens where you work or study.

Actions:

1. A blank presentation should still be on screen in **Normal** view. Select the **View** tab and click **Slide Master**.

2. The **Slide Master** is shown. Different **Master Slides** for the various layouts are listed on the left. The **Master Slide** for **Title and Content** is selected. Anything placed on this slide will appear on all **Title and Content** slides.

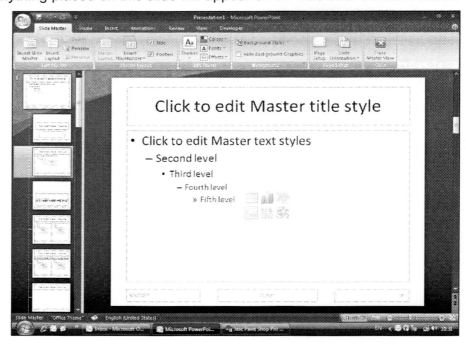

3. Select the main **Master Slide** at the top of the list. Anything placed on this slide will appear on <u>all</u> slides. In this guide, always make sure that this slide is selected when using **Slide Master** (it is not always the default).

continued over

Exercise 16 - Continued

4. Select the **Insert** tab and click the **Text Box** button from the **Text** group and drag the mouse to create a text box in the lower left corner of the **Master Slide**.

5. Type **Bacchus Tours**.

6. Select the **View** tab and click the **Normal** button. The text entered on to the master slide is shown, and it will appear on every slide added to the presentation, except any title slides.

Note: *Eventually, when you have finished creating a presentation, content on the **Master Slide** may be obscured by other material on the individual slides - graphics, charts, etc. It is always best to create the **Master Slide** before adding material to the individual slides.*

7. Select the **View** tab and click the **Slide Master** button, then select the top slide master on the left. In the main slide view, click on the text **Click to edit Master title style**. The box surrounding this text becomes dashed, showing that it is selected. This is another **text box**.

8. Click on the text **Click to edit Master text styles** to reveal another text box.

9. Click on the other smaller text areas at the bottom of the slide to reveal their text boxes.

10. Close the **Slide Master** by clicking the **Normal** button from the **View** tab.

11. In **Normal** view, the same two text boxes are displayed, but with default text in them. Any text added to these text boxes will be displayed on this slide only.

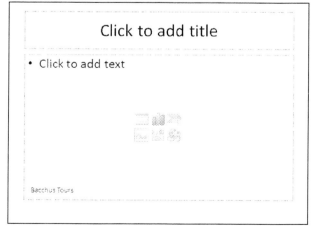

12. Leave the presentation on screen for the next exercise.

Exercise 17 - Bullet Levels

Guidelines:

Bullets are used to emphasise points in a slide. They can have any number of symbols, but in this guide only standard *PowerPoint* symbols will be used.

When text is entered on a slide *PowerPoint* assumes that it will be first level. The process of changing to a second level bullet is called **demotion**. Conversely, if text is at second level and you decide that is a main point, then it can be **promoted**.

In **Slide Master** view there are several levels of bulleted text available. This allows minor details to be made about major points.

Actions:

1. The blank presentation should still be on screen. Change to **Slide Master** view and select the main slide master. The levels of bullets can now be seen. There are **5** levels available.

2. The first bullet point is the most common, a round black circle. The second level bullet is actually a straight-line dash. These are the only two that will concern you, but notice the other bullets that are available.

3. Return to **Normal** view.

4. Click on the text ▪ Click to add text . Type in **This is the first point.**

5. Click the **Outline** tab in the **Slides/Outline** pane to change to **Outline** view.

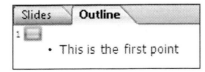

6. Right click on the text in the **Outline** pane to display a shortcut menu. Click **Demote**, ⇒ , from the menu.

7. The bullet changes to a dash, i.e. second level. Once **Demote** has been used, **Promote** becomes available. Right click on the text and select **Promote**, ⇐ .

8. Leave the presentation open for the next exercise.

Exercise 18 - Applying a Background

Guidelines:

When showing a presentation, it is difficult for the viewer to concentrate on the content of the slides if the background takes their attention. For this reason, the usual convention is to have the same background on each slide. The viewer then has an idea what to expect, and so is able to concentrate on the content of the slide and not the slide itself.

A background can be a plain colour, a colour gradient or pattern, a texture or an image. You will only be concerned with the first option.

A background can be applied to a single slide or to all slides. If it is applied to the **Slide Master**, it will automatically apply to all slides.

Actions:

1. A blank presentation is still on screen. You are to apply a single colour background to this presentation. Display the **Slide Master** view.

2. Select the top slide master so that any changes will affect all slides in the presentation. From the **Background** group on the **Slide Master** tab, click the **Background Styles** button, Background Styles .

3. Various preset styles are listed; but for now select **Format Background**. The **Format Background** dialog box is displayed.

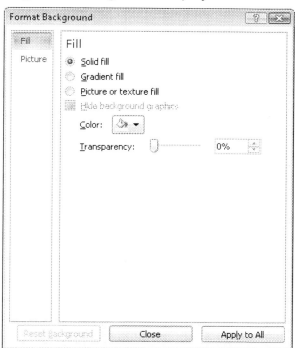

continued over

Exercise 18 - Continued

4. With **Fill** selected on the left, and the **Solid fill** option selected on the right, click the **Color** button, 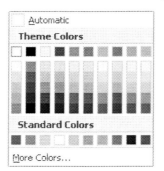, to view the colour options.

5. You can either make a choice from the coloured boxes or select a colour from **More Colors**. Select this option.

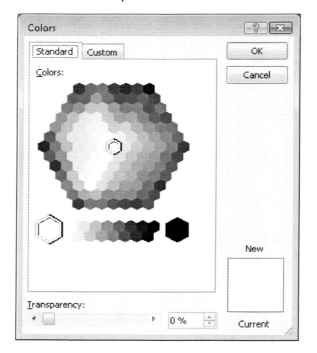

6. Any shades can be selected from here. The paler colours are near the centre, while the darker shades are nearer the outer edge. Select a pale colour by clicking on it. The chosen colour will appear as **New**.

7. Click **OK**. All the **Master** layout slides are instantly coloured. Click **Close**.

Note: To apply a background to a particular layout, select the required type and add the background. The background is only added to slides of that particular layout.

8. Change back to **Normal** view. The slide background shows the selected colour.

9. Leave this presentation on screen.

Exercise 19 - Saving a Presentation

Guidelines:

A presentation must be saved if it is to be used again. There are two main ways to save, depending on whether the presentation has been newly created, or whether it has previously been saved and given a name.

Actions:

1.　The new coloured presentation should still be on screen. Click the **Office Button** and select **Save As**. The **Save As** dialog box will then appear.

2.　The folder where the presentation is to be saved is shown at the top of the dialog box. Use the **Folders** view on the left to locate the supplied data folder. Choose a different location if required.

3.　The presentation must be given a name. Enter **Experiment** in the **File name** box (the highlighted text will automatically be deleted).

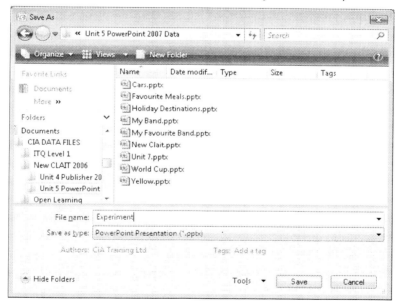

Note:　*A filename can be of any length. Choose a meaningful name but do not use any of the following characters: ><"*?:\ /;|.*

4.　Click the **Save** button, ⬚ Save ⬚, at the bottom right of the dialog box.

Note:　*A previously named presentation can be saved to the same location under the same name by clicking the **Save** button, 🖫, on the **Quick Access Toolbar**. When a new presentation is saved, clicking **Save** displays the **Save As** dialog box.*

5.　Notice how the name on the **Title Bar** has changed to show the new name.

6.　Leave the presentation on screen for the next exercise.

Exercise 20 - Adding a New Slide

Guidelines:

A new slide can be added to the presentation at any time and in any position.

Actions:

1. Using the **Experiment** presentation in **Normal** view, select the **Home** tab and click the arrow on the **New Slide** button in the **Slides** group.

2. Notice how the various layout options are displayed.

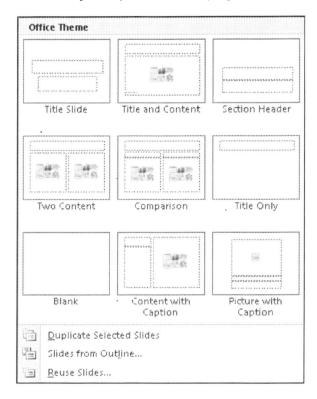

3. Click on the **Title and Content** layout.

4. The new slide, number **2**, has now been created with a title and the first bullet point. Notice that the **Status Bar** now shows **Slide 2 of 2**.

5. Notice that the background is the same as the previous slide. The colour and text box: **Bacchus Tours** applied to the **Slide Master** are on the new slide.

6. Save the changes using the **Save** button, 🖫.

7. Close the presentation by clicking the **Office Button** and selecting **Close**. As the presentation has just been saved it will close immediately.

Exercise 21 - Revision

1. Open the presentation **My Favourite Band**.

2. Change to **Normal View**.

3. Select to view the **Slide Master** for this presentation.

4. Click the **Background Styles** button and select **Format Background**.

5. Drop down the colours list and select **More Colors…**.

6. Change the background colour to a pale blue (make sure the **Transparency** box shows **0%**).

7. **Apply to All** slides, then **Close**.

8. Change to **Normal View** and check that the background has changed on all slides.

9. Add a new slide with a bulleted list (**Title and Content** layout).

10. Check in **Slide Sorter** view that the new slide is slide **4**. If not, move it to the end of the presentation.

11. Save the presentation as **Fans**.

12. Close the presentation.

Exercise 22 - Revision

1. Start a new presentation with a **Title Slide**.

2. Add a new **Title and Content** slide.

3. Change the background colour of the new slide only to pale pink (apply the background in **Normal View** and do not select **Apply to All**).

4. Save the presentation as **Pink**.

5. Close the presentation.

Section 4

Formatting Slides

By the end of this Section you should be able to:

Insert Text

Use Bullets

Change Fonts

Change Font Sizes

Use Bold, Underline and Italic

Apply Text Effects

Align Text

Replace Text

Use Cut, Copy and Paste

Exercise 23 - Adding Text to a Slide

Guidelines:

Once slides have been created or added, then the appropriate text can be entered. On many slides there are areas for a title and then for bulleted points to be listed.

The slide itself gives an indication on how text is entered, i.e. click to add title or text. The usual text entry rules apply, e.g. for capitals use <**Shift**> and the letter.

Actions:

1. Open the presentation **Yellow**.

2. In **Normal View**, display the first slide. This is the view where editing and adding of text takes place.

3. Move the mouse over the text **Click to add title** and click. The text disappears displaying the insertion point only.

4. Enter your name as the title.

5. Move the mouse over the first bullet point and click. Enter the following text, substituting the name of your town for the hashes: **I live in ####**.

6. Press <**Enter**> to end the first bullet point and start a new one. Type the text **I have lived here for #### years**.

7. This point is not needed. To delete it, place the cursor at the left of the text and click and drag to select the whole line. Press <**Delete**> to remove the text.

8. Click **Undo**, ↺, to replace the text. Another way of deleting text is to use <**Backspace**> or <**Delete**> to remove single characters.

9. Click in front of the word **here** in the bullet point. Press <**Delete**> until all text to the right of the cursor is gone.

10. Now press <**Backspace**> until all text to the left is gone.

11. Keep pressing <**Backspace**> until the bullet is removed and the cursor is at the end of the first bullet point. You will probably have noticed that it is much quicker to select all of the text and then delete it.

12. Save the presentation using the same name and leave on screen for the next exercise.

Exercise 24 - Text Formatting

Guidelines:

So that the text in the presentation is uniform throughout, any formatting is applied to the text on the **Slide Master**. It can be formatted in a number of ways, including changing the font, size, appearance, colour, etc. However, should you wish to draw special attention to text on one slide only, it can be formatted individually. This text must be selected before formatting can be applied.

Actions:

1. The presentation **Yellow** should still be on screen. Switch to **Slide Master View**, select the main slide master and click within one of the words in the text **Click to edit Master title style**.

2. The text box is highlighted. Click the **Home** tab and click on the **Font** drop down button, Times New Roma ▾. Move the cursor over various fonts and the effect will be seen on the slide. Click the **Arial Black** font from the list to apply it. You may need to use the scroll bars to move through the list.

Note: *If at any time a suggested font is not available, select an alternative.*

3. With the cursor in the same place, use the **Font Size** drop down list, 44 ▾, to change the size to **36**.

4. Click the **Increase Font Size** button, A▲, to increase the size of the font.

5. Click the **Decrease Font Size** button, A▾, to return the text to its original size.

6. Return to **Normal View** and note that **Your name** has changed to the selected Font.

7. View the main **Slide Master** again. Click within one of the words in the text **Click to edit Master text styles**.

8. Change the font to **Arial** and the size to **28**. Return to **Normal View**.

9. Check that the first bullet point has changed its font and size.

10. View the main **Slide Master** again. Select the text **– Second level**. Format this text so that it is **Arial**, but make the size **20**. This maintains continuity. The use of too many fonts detracts from the clear reading of the slide. Return to **Normal View**.

11. Leave the presentation on screen for the next exercise.

Exercise 25 - Using Second Level Bullets

Guidelines:

Second level bullets were briefly examined in Exercise 17. Remember these are used to give more detail about the main bullet point. The most important information should always be first level, followed by the extra item(s). An example is shown below:

When text is entered on a slide *PowerPoint* assumes that it will be first level. The process of changing to a second level bullet is called **demotion**. Conversely, if text is at second level and you decide that it is a main point, then it can be **promoted**.

These actions are carried out in the **Outline** pane in **Normal View**.

Actions:

1. The presentation from the previous exercise should still be on the screen. On the first slide, click at the end of the first bullet and press **<Enter>**. This adds another bullet.

2. Add the following text to the bullet, substituting the # for a number. This text is to be demoted to second level, as it is a minor point about where you live.

    My house has # bedrooms

continued over

Exercise 25 - Continued

3. Select the **Outline** tab on the left of **Normal View**.

4. In the **Outline** pane, right click on the text referring to bedrooms to display a shortcut menu. Click **Demote** from the menu. The text changes to second level.

5. As soon as there is second level text the **Promote** option becomes available.

6. Change the text back to first level by right clicking on it and selecting **Promote**.

7. Change it back to second level.

8. Leave the presentation on screen for the next exercise.

Exercise 26 - Applying Text Effects

Guidelines:

Various effects, such as bold, italic, underline, colour and shadow can be applied to text on slides. Effects can be applied to **Slide Master** text so that it is uniform throughout the presentation, or it can be applied to selected text on individual slides.

In this exercise below, you will use the latter.

Actions:

1. Click the **Slides** tab to display the **Slides** pane and select the second slide of the **Yellow** presentation. Click where indicated on the main slide display to add a title of **Relaxation**.

2. Select the text by clicking and dragging across it to highlight it. Display the **Home** tab and click the **Bold** button, **B**, in the **Font** group, to see the effect.

3. Click on the **Italic**, *I*, **Underline**, **U** and **Shadow**, **S**, buttons in turn.

4. Click on the buttons again in turn to remove the effect. Leave the **Italic** effect on when finished.

5. Enter **Reading** at the first bullet point.

6. Press **<Enter>** to create a new bullet. Type in **Listening to music** at this bullet.

7. Press **<Enter>** again and type in **Using my computer** at the third point.

8. The text box will have a dashed edge, ⬚. Any selected text or any text with the cursor within it, will be affected in this mode.

9. Click in **Reading**. Click on the **Underline** button. Only the word is affected.

10. Click on the edge of the text box so that it has a solid edge ⬚. Any formatting will now affect all of the text in the text box, an extremely quick and useful tool.

11. With the whole text box selected, click on the drop down arrow on the **Font Color** button, **A** ˅, on the **Font** group. The colour box appears.

continued over

Exercise 26 - Continued

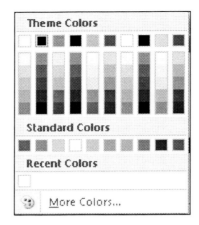

12.   The colours at the top are from the colour scheme for this background (**Theme Colors**). Click on any available colour.

13.   Open the colour box again. Click on **More Colors** and select the **Standard** tab. Choose a red colour from the honeycomb.

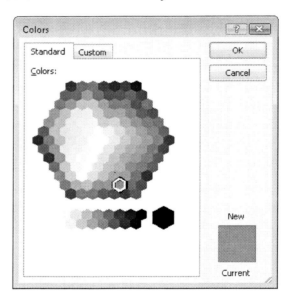

14.   Click **OK**. All text in the box is now red.

Note: If more than one effect is to be added to particular text, then it makes sense to do it in one action if possible.

15.   Select slide **1** and select the whole bulleted text box so that any changes made will affect all of the text in the box.

16.   Change the font, size, colour and effects to suit using buttons from the **Font** group.

17.   Save the presentation as **Personal** and close it.

Exercise 27 - Replacing Text in a Presentation

Guidelines:

Rather than finding and editing text manually, *PowerPoint* like many other applications has a replace option, making the process much quicker. This allows specified text to be replaced. **Replace** has an option to find and replace each occurrence individually or to **Replace All** occurrences.

Actions:

1.   Open the presentation **My Favourite Band**.

2.   Change to **Normal View**, if not already in use and select slide **1**.

3.   Select the **Home** tab and click [Replace ▾].

4.   In the **Find what** box enter **Band**. In the **Replace with** box enter **Group**.

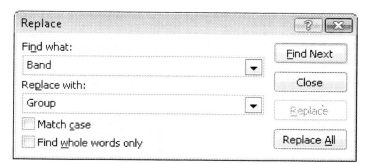

5.   Click **Find Next**. The first occurrence of the word **Band** is highlighted.

6.   Choose to **Replace** this occurrence. The word is replaced and the next occurrence of the word is highlighted.

7.   Select **Replace All** to replace the remainder of the occurrences within the presentation.

8.   At the prompt click **OK**.

9.   Close the **Replace** dialog box.

10. Save the presentation using the same name and close it.

Exercise 28 - Alignment

Guidelines:

Bulleted text is normally aligned to the **left**. This places all of the points neatly underneath each other.

The title for the slide could be left aligned, but is usually **centred**. This makes it stand out from the other text.

Text alignment can be altered on the **Slide Master**, which means it applies to all of the slides, or on individual slides.

Actions:

1. Open the presentation **World Cup**.

2. View the **Slide Master**.

3. At the moment the title text is centred and the bulleted text is left aligned. Click on the title text and select the **Home** tab. Look at the alignment buttons. The **Center** button appears highlighted, ▤ ▤ ▤ ▤.

4. Click the **Align Text Left** button, ▤, to see the difference.

5. Click on the first bullet. Once again view the alignment buttons. The **Left** alignment button is highlighted to show that it is selected, ▤.

6. Click the **Center** alignment button, ▤, to see the difference.

7. Display the **Slide Master** tab. The view can be returned to **Normal** by closing the **Slide Master**, click the **Close Master View** button. View the changes that have occurred on the slides.

8. Notice on **Slide 1** that the second level bullets have not been affected.

9. Leave this presentation open for the next exercise.

Exercise 29 - Using Cut and Paste

Guidelines:

The **Cut** and **Paste** commands allow text and other items, such as graphics, to be moved around a presentation from one place to another, quickly and easily. It is much quicker to cut and paste text, for example, than to delete and then retype it. When an item is cut, it is <u>removed</u> from its original location.

When copied or cut, text is placed in a temporary storage area known as the **Clipboard**. Up to **24** cut or copied items can be held on the **Clipboard**, which is common to all *Windows* applications.

Actions:

1.   With the **World Cup** presentation still open, in **Normal View**, view the first slide.

2.   Select the text **England** by clicking and dragging across it so that it becomes highlighted.

3.   Text selection is crucial here. – England is different from – England. Notice how in the second selection, the highlight extends beyond the end of the word and therefore includes the end of paragraph control. This is the preferred method and is the method expected here. If your spacing looks wrong after pasting then you have not used the preferred selection method.

4.   The **Cut** and **Paste** buttons are found on the **Home** tab, at the left of the **Ribbon**. The **Clipboard Launcher**, ▣, is at the bottom right of the group.

5.   Click the **Cut** button, ✄. The text is removed from the slide.

6.   Click at the end of **Grand Canary** and press **<Enter>**.

7.   Click the **Paste** button to place the cut text here. If an extra bullet is created, use <**Backspace**> to remove it.

8.   Move to slide **3**. Select the text **7ᵗʰ June - 6am Kick Off**.

9.   **Cut** the text.

10. Ensure the cursor is flashing before the **2** of **28ᵗʰ July**.

11. Click **Paste**. The text will be pasted and the spacing should be **OK**.

continued over

Exercise 29 - Continued

12.   Select **5th August - 12.30pm Kick Off** and cut it.

13.   Click the **Clipboard Launcher**, ▣; the **Clipboard** will appear as a **Task Pane** at the left side of the screen. An icon and text represents the cut item on the **Clipboard**.

*Note: As more items are cut or copied, they will also appear on the **Clipboard**.*

14.   Place the insertion point before the **2** of **20th June** and click on the **5th August** icon on the **Clipboard**. The text is placed in front of **20th June**. The **Clipboard** is useful if several items are to be pasted several times.

15.   Use **Cut and Paste** (and the **Clipboard**) to return the list of dates to the original correct order.

16.   Leave the **Clipboard** and the presentation open for the next exercise.

Exercise 30 - Using Copy and Paste

Guidelines:

Text or other items may also be **copied** to the **Clipboard**; when copied, the original is untouched. Copying and pasting text means that you don't have to spend time retyping it.

Actions:

1.   Using the **World Cup** presentation, on Slide **2**, select the text **Beck's Boots**, including the extra space at the end of the line.

2.   Click the **Copy** button, ▦. The icon for the copy has been placed on the **Clipboard**, but the original text remains in place.

3.   Place the insertion point at the start of the second bullet point.

4.   Locate the **Beck's Boots** icon on the **Clipboard** and click on it.

5.   The **Beck's Boots** text is repeated below the original as a new second line.

6.   Because the extra space at the end of the line (with the paragraph control) was copied, this should create a new line with **Sheringham's Shin** as line 3. If not, place the cursor in front of Sheringham's and press <**Enter**> to move it to a new line.

7.   Select **Boots** on the copied line.

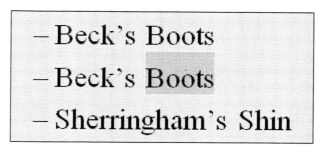

8.   Type in **Tours**. A new sponsor has now been added to the tour.

9.   Save the presentation with the same name and close it.

10. The **Clipboard** remains open. Click ✖ Clear All to clear the **Clipboard**, then ✖ to close the **Clipboard** task pane.

Exercise 31 - Revision

1. Open the presentation **Cars**.

2. In **Slide Master** view, change the title text to **Rockwell** font, size **54pt**. Make it **Bold** with a **Shadow**.

3. Change the first level text to **Harrington** font, size **40pt** and **Bold**.

4. Change the second level bullet text to **Harrington** font and size **28pt**.

5. Go to **Normal View**.

6. On slide **1**, select the text **Make 1** and type in **Ford**.

7. Replace the rest of the names with **Mercedes, Porsche and BMW**.

8. Save the presentation as **My Cars** and close it.

Note: A sample slide is shown in the Answers at the back of the guide.

Exercise 32 - Revision

1. Open the presentation **Cars**.

2. Replace all occurrences of the word **Make** with **Manufacturer**.

3. Select slide **2** and insert a new **Title and Content** slide.

4. Enter the title **Insurance Details**.

5. Add bullets as listed below:

> • Excess Fee £200
> • Cover Includes
> • Windscreens
> • All Mirrors
> • Damage

6. Demote the last three bullets to second level.

7. Save and close the presentation.

Note: A sample slide is shown in the Answers at the back of the guide.

Exercise 33 - Revision

1. Open the presentation **New Clait**.

2. Replace all occurrences of the word **Unit** with **Section**.

3. View the **Slide Master** for this presentation (make sure you have selected the main slide master on the left).

4. Change the title font to **Tahoma** and **Underline** it.

5. Change the size of the second level bullet font to **20**.

6. View slide **7** in **Normal View**.

7. Click after the word software and press **<Enter>**. Add the bullet point text:

    I use PowerPoint 2007

8. Demote this text to second level.

9. Close the presentation <u>without</u> saving.

Note: A sample of slide 7 is shown in the Answers at the back of the guide.

Section 5

Inserting Clip Art and Pictures

By the end of this Section you should be able to:

Insert Clip Art

Insert, Move and Resize Pictures

Use Graphic Tools

Exercise 34 - Inserting Clip Art

Guidelines:

Clip Art is a store of pictures that are available within all *Microsoft Office* products. They have several names, e.g. clipart, pictures, graphics, but all basically, mean the same thing. Any picture added in **Slide Master** view will appear on every slide.

The **Clip Art** task pane contains graphics, which are sorted into categories, so the appropriate clip can be found quickly. The quickest way to insert a graphic is simply to click on it in the **Clip Art** pane, although there are alternative methods.

Actions:

1. Open the presentation **Personal** (created in Exercise 26). Change to **Slide Master** view. Select the main **Slide Master** at the top of the list.

2. Select the **Insert** tab and click the **Clip Art** button. The **Clip Art** task pane appears.

3. In the **Search for** field, type **animals**.

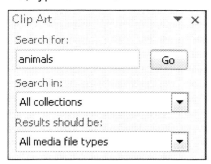

4. Click the **Go** button to see some graphics from this category. Some Clip Art examples are installed with *PowerPoint*. If you have an active Internet link, more examples will be available from the web.

5. Use **Search for** to look at some of the other categories of picture. You may need to use the scroll bar at the right to view more pictures.

6. Search for **people**, then choose a suitable representation of yourself (pick any graphic if none are particularly like you!).

7. Click on the relevant picture in the **Clip Art** task pane to insert it in the centre of the slide.

Note: Click and drag can be used to copy the picture from the task pane to any particular position on the slide.

8. The graphic will now be on the **Slide Master** with 'handles' around it. Leave this on screen and move on to the next exercise.

Exercise 35 - Moving and Resizing a Picture

Guidelines:

When a picture is added to a slide it may not be in the correct position or be of the correct size.

The technique used is the same whether the picture is added to the **Slide Master** or to an individual slide.

Actions:

1. The **Personal** presentation should still be on screen with **Slide Master** on view.

2. Click on the picture, if it is not already selected. White handles (small circles and squares) appear around the picture.

3. With the cursor inside the picture, ⬚. To move the picture, click and drag to move it around the screen. Release the mouse button when in the required position. Practise doing this.

4. The handles can be used to resize the picture. Move the cursor over the handles. When moving over a corner handle the cursor changes to a diagonal double arrow. The one in the top left corner looks something like this: ⬚.

5. When one of these handles is clicked and dragged, it will resize the picture proportionally. Click on the top left handle and drag up and left. The picture is made larger, but remains in proportion.

6. Move the cursor over the handle in the middle of the left side of the picture. It looks like this: ⬚.

7. Drag it to the left. This time the picture is resized in one direction only, giving the impression of being stretched like elastic.

8. Resize the picture to its original size or even a little smaller.

9. Move the picture to the bottom right corner.

10. Return to **Normal** view. Check both slides to see the chosen picture.

11. Close the **Clip Art** task pane.

12. Leave the presentation on screen for the next exercise.

Exercise 36 - Inserting a Picture from File

Guidelines:

Being able to insert a picture from file means that you are not reliant on the **Clip Art** provided by *Microsoft*. Pictures or logos saved in various formats can be added to slides.

Actions:

1. The **Personal** presentation is still on screen. View slide **2**.

2. Insert a new slide with a **Blank** layout. This will be slide **3**. Use the **Slide Sorter View** to check that it is in the correct position. If not move it to slide **3** position. The inserted picture added to the **Slide Master** will automatically appear.

3. Switch to **Normal View**.

4. Select the **Insert** tab and click **Picture**. The **Insert Picture** dialog box appears.

5. Make sure the supplied data folder, **Unit 5 PowerPoint 2007 Data** is shown. You will notice that only the picture files are displayed. The view shown here is **Medium Icons**.

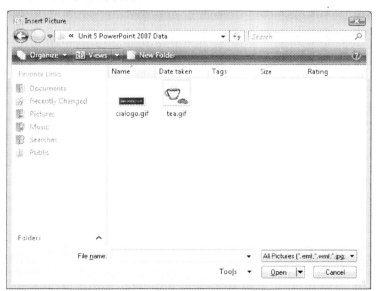

6. Click on the picture of the file **cialogo** to select it. Click [Insert ▼] to place the picture on the slide. The picture does not appear on other slides

7. Move it to the top left corner and resize it proportionally to be about half the width of the slide.

8. Save the presentation and leave it open.

Exercise 37 - Using Graphic Tools

Guidelines:

The **Shapes** tools allow drawings to be made directly on to a slide. The tools can only be displayed in **Normal** and **Notes Pages** views. The buttons relating to drawing are all available from the **Shapes** button.

Objects can be drawn by clicking on the appropriate button and then clicking and dragging on the slide. All objects have handles, similar to clip art, which can be used to reshape and re-size the drawing. When a shape is selected, the **Drawing Tools - Format** tab becomes available.

Actions:

1.   The **Personal** presentation is still on screen. Insert a new **Blank** slide at the end of the presentation.

2.   Select the **Insert** tab. In the **Illustrations** group, click **Shapes** to reveal the available shapes.

Note: *There is also a **Shapes** button in the **Drawing** group on the **Home** tab.*

3.   From the **Lines** area, click the **Line** button, then click and drag a line on the slide.

4.   Display the shapes again and click the **Arrow** button, then click and drag an arrow on the slide.

5.   The start and end style of arrows can be changed. Make sure the arrow line is selected. Display the **Format** tab and click Shape Outline, select **Arrows** and then **More Arrows**.

6.   From **End type** within the **Arrow settings** area, choose the **Oval Arrow**.

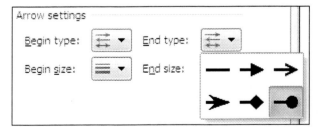

7.   Click **Close** to apply the style to the arrow.

8.   From **Shapes**, click the **Rectangle** button then click and drag to draw a rectangle anywhere on the slide, then use the **Oval** button (**Basic Shapes**) to draw an ellipse.

continued over

Exercise 37 - Continued

9. Practise drawing lines, rectangles, arrows and ovals (ellipses).

*Note: Holding down <**Shift**> while drawing an oval will create a circle. Holding down <**Shift**> while drawing a rectangle, will produce a square. Holding down <**Shift**> for lines or arrows will force them to be horizontal, vertical, or at a fixed angle.*

10. From **Shapes**, **Basic Shapes**, click on the smiley face, 😊. Click and drag to draw this image on the page.

11. Drawn images may be moved and resized like other objects. With the smiley face selected, click and drag a corner handle to change the size. Click and drag on any other part of the shape to move it.

12. Practise drawing shapes from the various selections.

13. When closed shapes (circles, rectangles, etc.) are drawn, they may be filled with a colour. This can be changed. Double click on the smiley face to display the **Drawing Tools - Format** tab.

14. Click the arrow on the **Shape Outline** button, [Shape Outline ▼], to see some suggested alternative colours for the shape outline.

15. Select a dark red shade from the **Standard Colors** on the palette.

16. Click the arrow on the **ShapeFill** button, [Shape Fill ▼], to see some suggested alternative colours to fill the shape.

17. From **Standard Colors**, select a bright yellow shade.

*Note: For a wider range of colours, select **More Fill Colors** or **More Outline Colors** from the palette.*

18. Select one of the drawn rectangles and click the arrow on the **Shape Fill** button. This time select **Gradient** and then click **More Gradients**.

19. The **Format Shape** dialog box is displayed. Gradients, textures, patterns and pictures can all be applied to fill shapes. Select **Gradient** fill, then click the **Preset colors** button, [Preset colors: ▼]. Select **Early Sunset** from the thumbnails (they all have **ToolTips**, it's the first thumbnail).

20. Click **Close** to see the effect.

21. Practise colour effects on other shapes then close the presentation <u>without</u> saving.

Exercise 38 - Revision

1. Open the presentation **Favourite Meals**.

2. View the **Slide Master**, ensuring the main slide master is selected from the left pane (**Default Design Slide Master**).

3. Open the **Clip Art** task pane.

4. Search for **Food** and insert an appropriate picture.

5. Resize it if it is too large and move it the bottom right corner.

6. On slide **2** the picture may overlap the bulleted text. Move the picture if necessary.

7. Add a new blank slide to the end of the presentation and use simple drawing tools to create the following shape.

8. Save as **Pictures** and close the presentation.

Note: A sample of the presentation is shown in the Answers at the back of the guide.

Exercise 39 - Revision

1. Start a new presentation with a **Title and Content** slide.

2. Add a new slide of the same kind.

3. View the **Slide Master**.

4. Change the background colour to pale pink.

continued over

Exercise 39 - Continued

5.   Open the **Clip Art Task Pane** and search for a clip relating to **cakes**.

6.   Make it an appropriate size and move it to the top right of the **Slide Master**.

7.   **Left** align the title text.

8.   View slide **1** in **Normal View**.

9.   Add the title **Tilly's Teas**.

10.   Add the bullets:

- Devon Cream Tea
- Scone
- Clotted Cream
- Jam
- Tea

11.   Make the last 4 points second level.

12.   Add further points:

- Yorkshire Tea
- Sandwiches
- Sausage Rolls
- Selection of Cakes

13.   Promote **Yorkshire Tea** to first level.

14.   Select the text **Yorkshire Tea** and all of its associated text. **Cut** the text.

15.   If any extra bullets have been created, remove them.

16.   Display slide **2**.

17.   Enter the title **Our Speciality** and paste in the cut text, removing any extra bullets if necessary.

18.   Insert the **tea** picture from the data files.

19.   Move it to an appropriate place on the slide and resize if necessary.

20.   With the picture still selected, click the **Copy** button, then immediately press the **Paste** button (a copied version of the cup of tea picture will appear overlapping the original).

21.   Move the copied picture next to the original.

22.   Save the presentation as **Teas** and close it.

Note: A sample of the presentation is shown in the Answers at the back of the guide.

Section 6

Slide Shows

By the end of this Section you should be able to:

Spell Check the Presentation

Apply Headers and Footers

Change Page Setup

Run the Presentation

Print Slides and Notes Pages

Print Handouts

Print Outline View

Exercise 40 - Spell Checking

Guidelines:

A presentation should be checked for spelling mistakes before it is shown. A spell checking function is available, which can either be used to check spelling as text is entered, or to check a complete presentation in one process.

Spell checker will only highlight words it does not have in its dictionary, it will not find incorrectly used words, e.g. **her** instead of **here**.

Actions:

1. Open the presentation **New Clait** and make sure the first slide is shown in **Normal View**.

2. Select the **Review** tab and click **Spelling** (or press <F7>). The spell checking process is started. A spelling mistake will be detected on slide **5**.

3. If possible, alternative spellings will be suggested. In this example only one suggested alternative is given. You have the option to **Ignore** the suggestion and leave the spelling as it is, or **Change** it to the selected word from the **Suggestions** list. Click **Change**.

4. The word is corrected and the next mistake will be highlighted if there is one. When all mistakes are changed or ignored a message will be displayed. Click **OK** to end the process.

5. Click the **Office Button** and then **PowerPoint Options** and the **Proofing** button. Make sure the **Check spelling as you type** option from **When correcting spelling in PowerPoint** is checked and click **OK**.

6. Display the last slide of the presentation and add a new **Title and Content** slide. Enter the first bullet point text as **Book yur course now**.

7. The word **yur** should be underlined in red to indicate a spelling error. Right click on it to see a list of suggested alternatives.

8. Select **your** from the list to replace the error.

9. Leave the presentation open for the next exercise.

Exercise 41 - Headers and Footers

Guidelines:

Certain standard information such as name, date, page numbers, can be added to every slide in a presentation using header and footer areas.

Actions:

1. With the **New Clait** presentation open select the **Insert** tab and click **Header and Footer**.

2. Check the boxes for **Date and time**, **Slide number** and **Footer**, and select the **Update automatically** option. The **Preview** area shows the position of these entries on the slide.

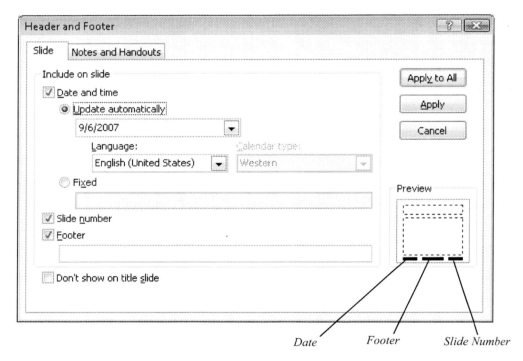

Date   Footer   Slide Number

3. Type your name in the **Footer** text box and click **Apply to All**.

4. Examine every slide in **Normal View**. Notice that every slide contains common information in the footer area with each slide having its own slide number.

5. Leave the presentation open for the next exercise.

Exercise 42 - Page Setup

Guidelines:

The size and orientation of the slides in a presentation can be defined from the **Page Setup** dialog box.

Actions:

1. With the **New Clait** presentation open select the **Design** tab and click **Page Setup**.

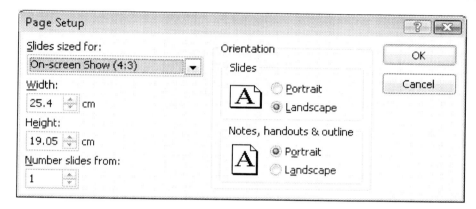

2. By default the slides are sized to fit a standard computer screen. Click the drop down arrow on the **Slides sized for** box to see the alternatives.

Note: When the **Custom** size is selected, the actual width and height of the slides can be set using the spinner boxes.

3. By default the orientation for slides is **Landscape** and **Portrait** for all other prints. Change the slide orientation to **Portrait** and click **OK**.

4. Examine the slides in **Normal** view. All the content is still present but the layout will be affected and some distortion of images may occur. If the final orientation is required as **Portrait**, it would be much better to design the whole presentation in this mode from the beginning.

5. There is an alternative method for changing the orientation without using the **Page Setup** dialog box. To change the slide orientation back to **Landscape**, click the **Slide Orientation** button in the **Page Setup** group of the **Design** tab and select **Landscape**.

6. Close the presentation <u>without</u> saving.

Exercise 43 - Running a Presentation

Guidelines:

The two most common reasons for creating a presentation are to produce printed handouts and to create a slide show. The slide show can be printed out as actual slides, projected from the computer on to a screen (with the appropriate equipment), shown on the Internet or as a show on the computer screen itself.

The order of slides in a presentation can be changed to suit a particular occasion or a particular audience.

Actions:

1. Open the presentation **Holiday Destinations**.

2. Change to **Slide Sorter View**. For the next showing of this presentation you have decided to show the Far Eastern destinations before America and Canada. Click on slide **3** and drag it so that it appears before slide **2**.

3. Select the **Slide Show** tab and look at the **Start Slide Show** group. There are options for running the slide show. It can be run from the beginning (first slide) to the end, or it can be run from the current slide to the end.

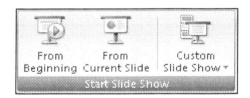

Note: *The third option is to run a custom show where only certain slides are selected to be shown. Custom shows are not covered at this level.*

4. Click the **From Beginning** button.

5. This presentation has not been set to run automatically, so each slide must be advanced manually. Click on the left mouse button to move to the next slide. The show will run in the order **Europe**, **Far Eastern**, **America and Canada**.

6. Once the show has completed a black slide will be shown with the following message: **End of slide show, click to exit.** .

7. Click the mouse button again to return to **Slide Sorter View**.

Note: *If the presentation is saved now, the revised slide order will become the order for the presentation the next time it is opened.*

8. Leave the presentation open for the next exercise.

Exercise 44 - Printing Slides

Guidelines:

Slides can be printed on separate pieces of paper for reference and storage.

Actions:

1. With **Holiday Destinations** still on screen from the previous exercise, in **Slide Sorter View**, select the second slide.

2. Make sure the printer is switched on and loaded with paper.

3. Click the **Office Button** and select **Print**. The **Print** dialog box appears.

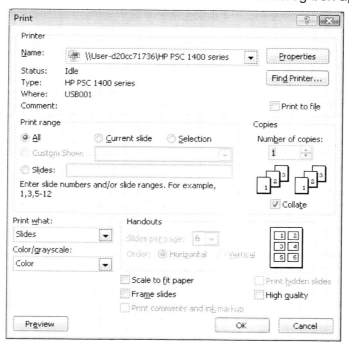

4. Check that the correct printer name is selected.

5. In the **Print range** area, the slides to be printed can be selected. Make sure that **All** is selected.

6. From the **Copies** area, ensure the **Number of copies** is set to **1**.

7. Make sure that **Slides** is selected under **Print what**.

8. Unless you have a colour printer and particularly want to see the colour effects, select **Grayscale** as the **Color/grayscale** setting.

9. Click **OK**. All slides will be printed, one on each page.

10. Leave the presentation open for the next exercise.

Exercise 45 - Printing Notes Pages

Guidelines:

A presentation can be printed in **Notes Page** view, i.e. a slide image with any added notes below. This could be useful as a script for the presenter during the public showing of the presentation.

Actions:

1. With **Holiday Destinations** still on screen from the previous exercise, make sure slide 2 is selected and click the **Office Button** and select **Print**.

2. From the **Print what** drop down list, select **Notes Pages**.

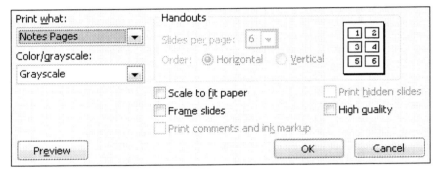

3. Click **OK** to print the notes pages.

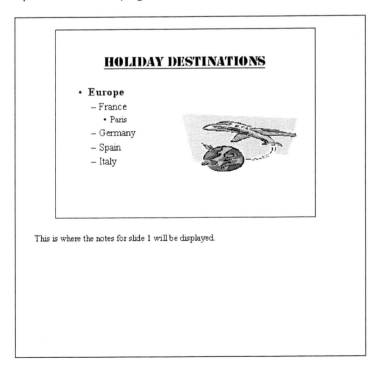

4. Leave the presentation open for the next exercise.

Exercise 46 - Printing Handouts or Thumbnails

Guidelines:

Handouts can be printed for an audience to follow as the presentation is running. They can use them for reference to remind them of the presentation. They have several slides on one printed sheet, in miniature, so giving rise to the name thumbnails, as they can be as small as a thumbnail.

Actions:

1. With **Holiday Destinations** still on screen from the previous exercise, in **Slide Sorter View**, click the **Office Button** and select **Print**.

2. From the **Print what** drop down list, select **Handouts**.

3. Drop down the list next to **Slides per page** and select **3**. The small preview at the right of this section shows how the printout will appear.

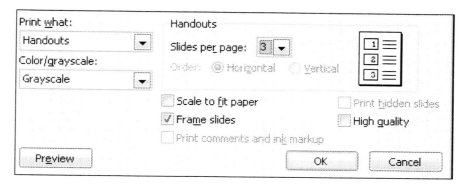

4. Click **OK** to print the handouts.

5. Leave the presentation open.

Exercise 47 - Printing Outline View

Guidelines:

A presentation can be printed in **Outline View** which shows only the text content of the slides in a presentation. Backgrounds, graphics and images are all omitted. This makes it easier to check the content for mistakes and continuity.

Actions:

1. With **Holiday Destinations** still on screen from the previous exercise, in **Slide Sorter View**, click the **Office Button** and select **Print**.

2. From the **Print what** drop down list, select **Outline View**.

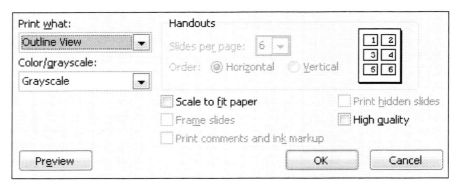

3. Click **OK** to print the content.

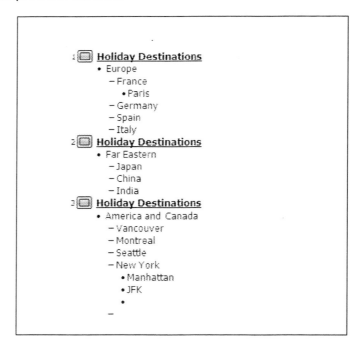

4. Close the presentation <u>without</u> saving.

Exercise 48 - Revision

1.   Open the presentation **World Cup**.

2.   Print out all of the presentation in slide format.

3.   Close the presentation.

Exercise 49 - Revision

1.   Open the presentation **My Favourite Band**.

2.   Print out in **Handout** format choosing to print **3** slides per page.

3.   Close the presentation.

Exercise 50 - Revision

1.   Open the presentation **New Clait**.

2.   Print out in **Handout** format choosing to print **9** slides per page.

3.   Close the presentation.

4.   **Exit** *PowerPoint*.

Answers

Exercise 31 - Revision

Cars

- Ford
- Mercedes
- Porsche
- BMW

Exercise 32 - Revision

Insurance Details

- Excess Fee £200
- Cover Includes
  - Windscreens
  - All Mirrors
  - Damage

Exercise 33 - Revision

Exercise 38 - Revision

Exercise 39 - Revision

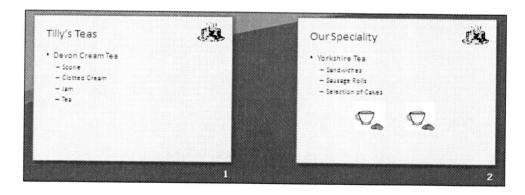

Glossary

Alignment	The arrangement of text or objects in relation to the slide or text box, e.g. left, centre, right, top, bottom.
Background	The colour of the slide.
Clip Art	A store of pictures that is available within all *Microsoft Office* products.
Copy	To create a duplicate of an object or section of selected text. Used when the copied item is to be duplicated.
Cut	To remove an object or section of selected text. Used when the item is to be moved to another location.
Demote	To move a selected section of text down one stage through a hierarchy of levels, e.g. title to subtitle.
Formatting	Changing the appearance of text, graphics, etc.
Outline Pane	A view of the presentation that allows text to be promoted or demoted.
Paste	Used after **Cut** or **Copy** to position the item (move or duplicate).
Presentation	A collection of slides used by a speaker as a visual aid.
Promote	To move a selected section of text up one stage through a hierarchy of levels e.g. subtitle to title.
Slide Layout	The type of slide, e.g. **Title Slide**, **Title Only**, **Title and Content**, etc.
Slide Master	This view is for adding items that are to appear on all slides in a presentation.
Slide Show	A preview of the presentation, with all effects, sounds, etc.
Slides	These make up the presentation, each refers to a specific area.
Text Effects	Formatting such as bold, italic, shadow, superscript, etc.
Thumbnails	Pictures that are displayed at reduced size, in order to save physical or storage space.
Views	Different ways of looking at slides.

Index

Record of Achievement Matrix

This Matrix is to be used to measure your progress while working through the guide. This is a self assessment process, you judge when you are competent. Remember that afterwards there is an assessment to test your competence.

Tick boxes are provided for each feature. 1 is for no knowledge, 2 is for some knowledge and 3 is for competent. A section is only complete when column 3 is completed for all parts of the section.

PowerPoint 2007

New CLAIT

Tick the Relevant Boxes **1**: No Knowledge **2**: Some Knowledge **3**: Competent

Section	No	Exercise	1	2	3
1 Fundamentals	1	Starting PowerPoint			
	2	The PowerPoint Screen and Ribbon			
	3	Opening a Presentation			
	4	Slide Show Basics			
	5	Closing a Presentation			
	6	Exiting PowerPoint			
2 Slide Views	8	Views			
	9	Using Slides View			
	10	Using Slide Sorter View			
	11	Saving an Edited Presentation			
	12	Closing an Unsaved Presentation			
3 Presentations	15	Creating a Blank Presentation			
	16	Using Slide Master			
	17	Bullet Levels			
	18	Applying a Background			
	19	Saving a Presentation			
	20	Adding a New Slide			
4 Formatting Slides	23	Adding Text to a Slide			
	24	Text Formatting			
	25	Using Second Level Bullets			
	26	Applying Text Effects			
	27	Replacing Text in a Presentation			
	28	Alignment			
	29	Using Cut and Paste			
	30	Using Copy and Paste			
5 Insert Clipart & Pictures	34	Inserting Clip Art			
	35	Moving and Resizing a Picture			
	36	Inserting a Picture From File			
	37	Using Graphic Tools			
6 Slide Shows	40	Spell Checker			
	41	Headers and Footers			
	42	Page Setup			
	43	Running a Presentation			
	44	Printing Slides			
	45	Printing Notes Pages			
	46	Printing Handouts or Thumbnails			
	47	Printing Outline View			

Other Products from CiA Training

CiA Training is a leading publishing company, which has consistently delivered the highest quality products since 1985. A wide range of flexible and easy to use self teach resources has been developed by CiA's experienced publishing team to aid the learning process. These include the following materials at the time of publication of this product:

- **Open Learning Guides**

- **ECDL/ICDL & ECDL/ICDL Advanced (ECDL Foundation Qualification)**

- **New CLAIT, CLAIT Plus & CLAIT Advanced (OCR Qualification)**

- **CiA Revision Series**

- **ITQs (Industry Standard Qualification)**

- **e-Citizen (ECDL Foundation Qualification)**

- **Trainer's Packs with iCourse**

- **Start IT (City & Guilds Qualification)**

- **Skill for Life in ICT (Industry Standard Qualification)**

- **iCourse - Course customising software**

We hope you have enjoyed using our materials and would love to hear your opinions about them. If you'd like to give us some feedback, please go to:

www.ciatraining.co.uk/feedback.php

and let us know what you think.

New products are constantly being developed. For up to the minute information on our products, to view our full range, to find out more, or to be added to our mailing list, visit:

www.ciatraining.co.uk